The Lunatic Moon

Chaaru Bhattacharyya

Ukiyoto Publishing

All global publishing rights are held by

Ukiyoto Publishing

Published in 2024

Content Copyright © Chaaru Bhattacharyya

ISBN 9789360492052

All rights reserved.

No part of this publication may be reproduced, transmitted, or stored in a retrieval system, in any form by any means, electronic, mechanical, photocopying, recording or otherwise, without the prior permission of the publisher.

The moral rights of the author have been asserted.

This is a work of fiction. Names, characters, businesses, places, events, locales, and incidents are either the products of the author's imagination or used in a fictitious manner. Any resemblance to actual persons, living or dead, or actual events is purely coincidental.

This book is sold subject to the condition that it shall not by way of trade or otherwise, be lent, resold, hired out or otherwise circulated, without the publisher's prior consent, in any form of binding or cover other than that in which it is published.

To Anyone who relates to my work...

Contents

The lunatic moon.	1
A poet's rant	3
A morbid romance	5
A translation	7
Leaks	9
A morbid self-discovery	11
The reason why I fall in love with people who live far away	13
First glance	15
Rejuvenation	17
We accept the love we think we deserve	18
The terror of intimacy	20
A lover in third person	21
Rainbow in my eyes	23
Since you've been gone	24
Killing loving, loving killing	25
Captive love	26
Grief	27
At least for a while you stayed	29
Love and time	31
Russian nesting dolls of pain	33
A horror story	36
The old children	38
One must imagine Sisyphus happy?	40

Insanity	44
Before the war comes	48
When the world closes its eyes	50
For the candle of dreams	52
Two sides of the same coin	54
A genocide and the mountains	56
My dear mother nature	58
After the storm	60
An eerie welcoming cemetery	62
The sea tastes like tears	65
A realization	67
The oblivion	68
I exist since the beginning of time	70
About the Author	72

The lunatic moon.

A lunatic moon dances,
The stars sink into themselves in its impact,
And a grey night clogs everyone's nostrils.
A lunatic moon dances,
Its black wings trigger a fatal tornado,
Drilling through all that ever was and ever will be.
A lunatic moon belts loud,
And the birds wake up in a jolt, startled.
The lunatic moon crashes on the barren meadows,
The impact sends a crack straight through its heart.
The Lunatic moon crumbles like a porcelain ball,
Its broken shards rise and fall like a fountain of glass
Piercing my skin,
Creating a bloodbath of horror imageries,
That purifies my eyes blanketed in years old cobwebs.
The lunatic moon embeds into my cerebrum,
Through my spine, in and around my veins,
Swelling like a sculpture,
Till I burst open,
Like a meteor shower of desperate cries.

The blood that drips down, the flesh that hangs out,

The bone that juts out, the veins that tangle up,

Consolidates and rises up and down,

In synchronisation with a fast pulse,

Into an intense menagerie of broken words, hasty phrases,

Oddly strung together by random punctuations.

The Lunatic moon breathes through it all,

Harbouring a catharsis that saves me on delirious evenings.

A poet's rant

Hurt me, hurt me like a mosquito dies
Splashed on the wall
In a single blow.
Hurt me, hurt me like red orange leaves
Leave its tree
To fall on the ground.
See me, see all of the pain
Trickle down my fingers
And fall drop by drop on the paper
Drawing words weaved together in despair.

Hurt us, hurt us all like a knife on butter
See it all drooling out of our frozen mouths,
Stained in red, flooding pages in the shape of consequences.
See us, see it all burn ablaze
Kerosene hands lighting a flame
Smothering you auburn.
Hurt us, hurt us all like a wound
Rubbed in salt

See it all pouring out like bloody mary
Out of our eyes
Could you see? Could you comprehend?
Hurt us only to immortalize your cruelty.

A morbid romance

I see the morbid waves hit my frail backbones,
From the void between comets,
Like a hungry tide, coiling around my shaky feet,
A python from the chambers of a grey psyche.
Thousand feet tall convection currents,
Pulls me round and over and under,
Dipping me in blood struck mud of careful whirlpools,
A gallery of complex carbons,
fight in my skull.
I dash away in a delusion of reprieve,
But Alas!
I'm getting sucked below,
In quicksand through portals from times long gone.

Before I exhale to end it all for ever and all,
My finger dances with ink on empty pale paper -
To rage against the void, the cobwebs and quicksand,
The blood and the tide,
Romance it all in symmetry and planned asymmetry,

Till then I can rest in comfort, - underwater,
Breathless, with edema,
In the tsunami of delirious screams.

A translation

Red light paints the canvas on my eyes,

In spooky hues and mystery shapes,

Of familiar dread and expired epiphanies.

I see an omen, dark and translucent

Hanging from the ceiling,

Three dimensional shadows,

Prickles my skin,

Like vampire nails in graveyards of dead poets.

The heart between my ribs,

Swell and shrink faster than my lungs can keep up to,

They're not mine,

Only puppets on strings,

Moved by grizzly hands that clasps round my windpipe,

I learn how to scream in silent loudness.

The world tumults on the way to the sink,

Cold tentacles trap my ankles from beneath the floors,

Sculpts ancient runes on my flesh.

Time stretches in and out,

While the chaos drools out of my eyes,

Like boiled water,
Exaggerated metaphors on a poets scribbles,
Words litter like dead scales of a lithe snake,
An attempt at translating the shrieks inside.

Leaks

Can you place your hand firmly on this open wound on my body to keep all my insides from spilling out?

Can you put a zip on all the gaping wounds on my body? Because I'm spilling out,

Slowly, steadily, - painfully.

Blood soaked rivers draining out of me with my organs like vessels in it.

All i am, however unknown, falls out of me,

I am becoming an abode of void,

that echoes the hollering of bygones.

I'm losing myself in streams of unconsciousness.

Hurry up, and hold me, nurse me,

Like a fallen soldier in a war am i.

Can you put it all inside my body cavity and make me feel whole again?

Shove it all, -cotton, wood, plastic,- anything inside my empty skeleton

So that i become a ghost of what i was.

Alas! It's too late.

My limp body lies in the morgue,

Like a battered popped balloon.

Can you take me in your arms and float me in the river at least?

I want to see me plump and soft before the fire incinerates me.

A morbid self-discovery

A lullaby rings in my ears with a eerie sound box,

And I hum to it as the moonless night trickles into the gathered dust on the kitchen shelf.

Under the blanket, a derelict and gothic castle echoes its melody,

As bats quit their slumber and fly out into the smoke out of a weary chimney.

The weed and vines in its wall's cracks create a soft bed,

Where I lie on my back and my eyes look up into ceiling,

From where a corpse hangs down low, cold and mangled.

My veins swell and bursts out black liquids,

They run through the vents and pour out into an open skull that used to fit on my neck.

East winds from the whispering woods howl through the corridors against the bloodstained pillars.

They quiver and tear apart the cobwebs hanging from the corners,

The cobwebs that treasure deadly secrets and dead skin flakes of victims of unspoken crimes.

I fall over on my side on the dirty marble floor only

to catch a glimpse of the form that is now mine,

On a broken mirror, tall and stained on the crumbling walls.

I see a doll in my reflection, left alone in a forgotten toy basket in an abandoned house.

Its tangled hair catches dust and wide lifeless eyes stare out into the oblivion.

Its carefully manufactured smile, small and gentle creeps my ceramic skin,

As I taste old clotted blood on my tongue under the smile.

The lullaby echoes like a muffled scream as my voiceless scream flood my hollow insides.

I have no pulse, no breaths, no rhythm, no senses.

My body lies lifeless on a deserted floor in a castle under the blankets,

As the moonless night overpowers dawn for an eternal darkness.

The reason why I fall in love with people who live far away

Distance, I felt it soon between my skin and the air that touches it.

My body didn't make sense to me.

Distance, hollowing and corrosive, I had it seep between my mother and me.

We stand facing each other with it between us.

Distance, silent and eerie, I find it chip in between my father and me,

Its weight muffling words in my throat.

Distance, it looms large beside people I call my friends and me,

I sit on the bench with an inanimate friend.

Distance, I found it increasing day by day like an impending doom.

I was unaware, I don't remember much.

Distance finds its way between my memories and my consciousness,

I am detached from my past.

Distance spreads like a virus until it isolates me from the world,

Distance invites loneliness over to my house as its

plus one.

I grow with them in my room.

I grow familiar with them.

Now I'm grown.

Distance has invaded my bones and flesh,

Even if I want touch, distance resides in my skin now,

I can't touch or be touched through distance lying under my skin.

Distance has become so integral that I unknowingly only fall in love with people who live far away.

Distance has become a part of me.

I have become a part of distance.

Somewhere through the maze of passing time,

We fused as one -

An alloy of airy distance and fleshy form

I haunt myself like a ghost.

First glance

I saw a light in your eyes,

Mellow and soft illuminating the dark room inside my empty ribs,

I was waiting for an impending doom,

Rehearsing the same lines,

Recycling the same restlessness between my ventricles.

You smiled at me and the pressure within me found a way out,

Through my pores, entangling with the stories you weave,

I don't know how to sit with this feeling

It builds slowly and softly, firmly and steadily

Like a vine on a wired fence around the walls I build.

Your name rings like an echo in a cave,

And I find myself drowning in its frequency.

I keep revisiting the moments you gave me,

When you looked across the yard,

When you talked to me like a wave crashing the shore,

I live them again,

I sit beside us, looking at you,

Admiring and adoring,
I don't know how to sit with this growing feeling,
It bathes me in a starlight too far away,
I'm lost.

I'd reside in the initial spark of the match,
Then it is burnt to crisp, and tired ashes fall around me.
I'd run away before that.
I'd control my quench for the intense flutters,
So that i can run away from the languid fatigue,
Before it sucks away the life from you, and us.

Rejuvenation

I am made of memories -

Memories of you dripping down my neck, and under my chin,

That stir a cold heart into existence, beating frantically,

Climbing up the stairs of life into your endless eyes -

The eyes that reeks into my dead skin cells, that glows in a tired night's gloom,

And pours a potion of rejuvenation inside my rib cage.

Your hands run through the air that chokes my neck,

Like an athlete's daft strokes, sweeping the grails away

As I breathe - one, two, three, four - in your fragrance

Sharper and sweeter than the sea salt in the rain.

I feel the memories tingle my pores, giving me goose bumps

As my heart bursts open into shards of red crystals

Varnished in your touch, cutting me open, yearning, and searching

For you, and your hazel eyes, where I curl up in the tufts of your hair, -

Rejuvenating.

We accept the love we think we deserve

A healing ointment stings the wound before it heals,

Like your love fries my naked burnt flesh,

Before it seeps into my ventricles and curls up cosily,

In a safe home.

My eyes dream of an effervescent glow,

And shuts itself immediately when the glow materializes into existence.

I wear sunglasses, to shade my eyes accustomed to only dreaming.

So when you reach out your hand through the glowing halo,

And hold my stripped bare burnt flesh,

It stings, and aches,

But I love the pain,

Seconds after I yank my hand away from you.

I look at you,

My body breaks apart at the seams -

A part of it flows into you,

Another part retreats back,

Like an alternative undertow of ebb tides and flood

tides,

As my feet stand admist the circling current.

I look at you

And fall on your frame,

My entire body aches before it quietens down to a comfortable silence,

It fries and boils into a warm embrace,

As your essence drips down my white eyes,

My red bruises and fatigued muscles,

Like a blanket wrapped over cold ribs.

The terror of intimacy

Love pricks my nape,

Electrocuting my entire body,

Hair to toe in a blue streak of light.

One hand, I reach forward for some warmth

But when I'm reciprocated,

The ground beneath caves into an abyss akin to my chest

Where i fall, not a soft landing,

With a concussion on my left brain.

It's a wonder how hands are made to interlock with each other,

Yet made perfectly to circumcize a knife,

That stabs in the back in a delicate embrace.

Love is a fatal dealer with a promise of warmth,

And a risk of heartbreak,

So the terror of intimacy spreads through my veins

Like a poison ivy,

Inebriating my soul to a fatal overdose.

A lover in third person

Elios met Patroclus,

beyond a river's turbulent nymphomaniac waves,

To talk of lost beloved men,

Like berries dripping honey,

Or sparkly sting of a sip of wine.

Too elegaic, in its pristine poignancy,

to tug at the rusty hearstrings of my tired cage.

I close my eyes to soften the concrete clench around my neck,

Lightly raising my chin to dissolve in Marianne's paintbrushes,

As they paint her cutting love,

I yearn to feel it, too alien for my withered skin.

The forbidden lovers beneath a sky ,

Preserved in

Words and pixels, in art and dreams

They gnaw at my cold steel walls of paralysis.

For, I am a lover as long as it's a wistful poem,

I am a lover as long as it's a raging violin

I am a lover till the poetry ends, music stops, curtains fall,

Then I'm another concrete lump resembling human flesh.

Another maudlin silhouette of lovelessness and ennui.

If you need to find me,

You can find me in the confluence of yearning and losing the same intimate tenderness,

Fated to be a distant observer, never a participant.

If you need to find me,

Meet me at the bottom of the mountains too jarred for me to climb over,

For a peck of kiss,

Or a few honey glazed nights,

Only for something in me to be shrunken back soon enough,

Like Eurydice, when you turn around to reach for me.

Rainbow in my eyes

There's a stinging spark in my chest,

Akin to golden sunshine glimmering in a new day's grace.

Hope, bright like a child's smile,

Of promises and love,

Splashes on my bones and flesh

Like dew drops on glass blades,

Showering in grace.

From the other side,

Dark omens laugh at me,

Of apprehensions and familiar sabotage,

When the sun goes down,

And night arrives with its lucid lunatic nightmares,

Trapping me in a cage,

A wall between you and me.

Clouds and sun,

There's a rainbow in my eyes,

Reach for me,

If I dissolve like Eurydice

When Orpheus turned around.

Since you've been gone

Since you've been gone,

I've lost the ability to write poetry

Because you were my poetry - turbulent and passionate.

I lost my poetry; I can only fall like autumn leaves,

Fall on the harsh cold pavement,

With a thousand bruises all over my skin,

Tainting me with colours of grief.

The universe contracts in my pupils

I can't see it anymore in your eyes,

For your eyes don't meet mine anymore.

Like a forbidden curse, memories fall in 37 tears.

The scars on my heart open wide bleeding out all the confessions of love,

That we shared in a trance,

Now I'm hopeless and helpless

Wondering if the extravagance of romance

Is only a precursor to a fatal death.

Killing loving, loving killing

A flower was given to me with love and care

And once again i stepped over it, killing it with all menace,

Accidentally? Who knows?

The love letters trampled in my dustbin ask,

"Are you better at killing than loving?"

And i stare speechless for I fear I'm the former, -

A killer dressed as a daydream .

Love is a mayhem while the blood in my fingers don't wash off.

All the flowers I have trampled over lie sound and bare for me to witness

My own crime.

Love is a mayhem and I am letting feathers fly off into space that i named love.

Captive love

There is a glimmer in my chest
Toned in greys and shadows
With a hopeless cry,
I named it love.
Love fills me up, head to toe,-
Replacing the blood in my veins,
But my heart is too fragile to pump all this love.
All this love in me has no place to go,
Save for the eyes in my face.

Soon, this love bulges out my body
Eating my flesh, slowly, like a sadist predator.
Oh, captive love in my ribs,
Sing me a lullaby,
To soothe the wounds you inflict with your two-faced knife.

Grief

On a cool December morning,
I wake up from a violent dream
Only to find grief sitting by my bed,
Quietly smiling at me.
In the breakfast table she spills over my bread
Meandering around boiled eggs
As i swallow all of it down my scarred throat.
I try to talk and words turn into tears
Falling out of my eyes.
I grab my keys and sit in the car
Only to find grief drives the car;
I'm only a passenger drowning in a pool of blood.
Grief takes me to graveyards
That look like a paradise
Like the only bearer of some warmth
That melts into loneliness.
Grief sits by my side on an empty park bench
Screaming with me,
Kissing me in a morbid romance.

Grief holds my hand and I hold her
She woos me and I fall in love.
Grief takes over me
And i die in her arms,
Safely, quietly, happily
In a warm embrace
On a cold December night.

At least for a while you stayed

I stand by a sea on grainy soft sand, barefoot.

People come like anticipatory waves from the horizon.

I stare at them running towards me, in a steady firm pace.

They hit the shore, crawling around my feet,

In a soft yet passionate embrace.

I breathe through my skin,

Inhaling their scent, knowing each cell, closely.

Then they tug away and retreat back into the unknown,

In the same steady firm pace,

Leaving me with wet feet, pieces of them,

Etched on my skin, as i stand, longing.

They dissolve amidst the grey horizon.

The cycle continues,

Leaving me wetter each time.

In between their arrival and retreat,

I breathe deeply to sink in whatever pieces of them I find meanwhile.

Maybe, In between the arrival and retreat lies all that matters about this cycle.

In between, I smile knowing well enough, I'd cry soon.

I console myself-

At least the waves chose my feet to embrace,

For a while.

At least for a while you stayed.

Love and time

I see my father struggling to carry bags of groceries
Up the stairs,
The spider hands of age stain him in sweat
And I wonder
How love still remains bulletproof from time's pistol
Like a buttered knife
That threatens to cut you in half, happily.

I see new grey hairs in the locks of my mother's hair
Covering her face,
The brown of the henna fails to stop the clock's hands
And I wonder
How love is a precursor to grief and we know that
Yet we love;
Like a foolish soldier we rage on in love, happily.

I worry time is an enemy love fights till eternity
I worry love is a violence we partake in
I worry we are a prisoner bound in time,

While time passes watching fathers and mothers turning old

Beside a clock that ticks in the dead silence of the night.

Russian nesting dolls of pain

Mother, if you look in the mirror under the dim yellow lights at 2 am,

Do you ever feel like you're a slightly distorted, less violent version of your own mother?

That you're made of the same broken shards of her tears, only in a different light?

Or that the blood you pump is tainted in that same weary fluid in her womb when you resided in her, in search of a home that she didn't have too?

Your words, your gaze, your voice reverberates her angry stance,

Polished and garnished into an ugly blade of decades of oppressed pain,

Mother, your hands do not wash the blood she painted you with.

Mother, my hands tremble for I see that blood trickling into my veins too,

Slowly, and steadily, slithering like a python in its firm calm embrace.

The pain shivers me head to toe, flowing like an eternal river since the beginning of time,

From mother to daughter, from daughter to mother,

In a gyrating loop of a repeated motiff,

And we're both stuck here, mother.

Mother, when I stand in front of the mirror, I see my reflection tainted in yours,

Your reflections tainted in your mother,

Outlined and filled in a repeated motiff of hurt and pain and regrets,

And an unbridled rage lodged in a brittle shell of love.

Mother, are we russian nesting dolls of pain, with our mothers inside our form?

I crash on the floor and you come out of my broken shell only to open your dusty lid and show me your mother inside.

Hey mother, did your mother's love burn you like stepping into lava too?

For, I see you mouthing my words unconsciously, unknowingly, unintentionally,

As I do yours, when you cry at night spilling out all the lost happiness you could've not lost if your mother knew better,

That I could've not lost if my mother knew better than what she knew to be better.

And I cry out asking why did you not know better but this hollow sky answers only with rain,

Mother, how could you have known better?

Mother, I hold your hand and my body shrieks coldness and hotness simultaneously,

My brain overwhelms itself in understanding the contrasting extremes,

As I look at your fiery eyes and find a hurt child only.

Mother, we compare lives as if we're commodities in competition in a market,

When we're just like each other yet so different and far apart yet so close,

My head spins to make sense.

Mother, I was born before my birth, in your scars, the moment you did.

Mother, I do not know what can satiate this pain,

But mother, I need you to see me, see me, see me.

For I cannot.

A horror story

On a quiet night,
The moon hides half of its face in the clouds,
And the moonshine reeks into my room
Through the windowpane,
Shining silently on a blob of darkness
I call memories.

Slithering like snake,
The memories drip down the side table,
Flow beneath my feet,
Sending a crisp feeling down where it touches me.
On a quiet night,
Memories become an ocean of oil
And I don't know how to swim.

The hollow abyss in my chest
Is now full to the brim
With blobs of memories toned in dark magenta.
They spill out of my cornea, my nostrils,

The pores on my skin, the corner of my lips.
On a quiet night,
Memories lash out at me
And i let it skin me alive.

The old children

I see old children - battered and tattered in grown bodies,

Mimicking adult lives.

They're trudging along the bridges, the streets, the pavements,

Like puppets on worn out strings, - strings held in the daft cunning hands of memory's omens.

I see old children - screaming and bleeding cramped in small hearts,

Reaching out to tomorrow with a hundred unhealed bruises.

They're talking, walking, smiling and nodding just like animated corpses, -

Trapped in the calculated chaos of a being called life.

I see old children - shoved and put aside by the weight of adult bodies

Suffocating in the haunted house of an adult skeleton.

The old children seek a crevice through the eyes of worn out people

From the inside, looking out, -

For air and light to breathe and assimilate.

How the old children want to live,

Trapped in the body of suicidal minds!

One must imagine Sisyphus happy?

Somewhere over the rainbow,
You can hear voices in a choir,
singing these words -
"Focus on the present.
Be mindful of the current senses.
The immediate moment."
So I close my eyes and look for
5 things to see,
4 things to touch,
3 things to hear,
2 things to smell,
1 thing to taste.
I had hoped to see a book,
a pillow to touch, or hear birds chirping,
inhale lavender perfume
and taste a sweet candy.
But I was met with a vision of a world caving in,
The sense of crumbling bones beneath a truck,
The scream of a hungry terrified child,

The smell of fresh blood from their wounds,

taste salty tears and sweat of silhouetted figures struggling to keep up with the rehearsed speech of a President.

I can't help it.

Somewhere over the clouds,

I have heard angels sing,

"The past is gone.

The present is here.

You can only affect the Now."

But angels don't live here on Earth.

How would they know what works here?

This isn't a silky smooth existence unlike that on the clouds.

By the time I can recognize the present,

it has already tumbled into the past

The future is here already.

The immediate moment is only an illusion

to make me feel like I have a false sense of control over time.

Somewhere over the Jet plane,

I hear them echo,

"You're not alone.

We're all struggling the same."

Do they hope to make me feel relieved by stating how I'm not 'crazy' for feeling this way?

No it doesn't help.

I wish I was 'crazy' instead.

I never wanted this to be normal.

I never hoped for this to be the baseline of our existence as a collective being.

I wish it was all just a chemical imbalance.

I wish it was all an anomaly in the brain,

corrected by medications.

Maybe they don't want us to find out that it's not all just a chemical imbalance.

They, who make us dance like a puppet from

the linen covered sofa,

watch us do the right thing for us,

only to turn against each other and die.

They just sigh and move on.

Please don't pathologize my thoughts.

My existence.

Call it a disorder, a syndrome, an illness,

When it seems like this was how it was meant to be all along,

given the malfunctioning world we breathe in,

the systems we've trapped ourselves into.

It's difficult to imagine Sisyphus happy.

It's almost unjust to hope Sisyphus to be happy.

Insanity

You laugh at my scars carved out of pain

Like they're a scaffolding of shame,-

Crime in a shell of raised flesh.

You ask me "why would you ever hurt yourself?"

When all i long to hear is, "how much pain did you feel that you chose this?"

Curiosity without empathy pierces my scars deeper than any blade could ever,

And I feel naked in scrutinizing disappointed eyes.

Death haunts my dreams in breathless nights,

When everything closes in on me,

And you only see me dying,

Not the frantically beating heart that is fatigued-

So so so fatigued that even love couldn't save it.

You remind me of guilt, of shame,

That people's love should bind me back,

But all that binds me is emptiness garnished in chilling pain.

You fail to see how the pain and hurt cuts across my skin before the blade does.

The blade has been my refuge and the stories around each wound,

Rises against my skin like an exposed genital.
You pull the trigger, the bullet runs through them,
Fresh and clear in invisible blood.
You do not see it, or anything at all,
Only the visible wounds you're scared of,
Can't you see they scare me too in anguish, in despair.
You think it's funny, strange,-
That I mark my body out of jest,
When all the gaping wounds do is burst out the piling up agony inside,
As a last resort like a balloon filled up at its limit.

You wonder, "what's the agony all about?"
When all I long to hear, "the agony is so real, I see you."
You don't understand like you're not supposed to,
I know, I know it all, and how different is threatening to you,
But my eyes still well up in tears I must hide to satiate you.
"Pain is inevitable" you say, "You must know better."
"We all have pain, why would you kill yourself then?"
And I stare helplessly at your face, not knowing the answer myself.

Death has befriended me on lonely delirious nights and my head is plagued in its smell,

How do I make you see living is like slow poisoning.

But my explanations appear to you as justifications and excuses,

Not as a cry for help.

And you're not helping,

Only putting the axe over my body, over and over again

Hurting me in newer places.

All those invisible scars elude your vision,

How can the criminal remember the crime?

You say, "we all have gone through the same."

While flashbacks of traumatic days pass my eyes

And I feel guilty again for being haunted by them,

For it's normal and common, and I must get over it.

When trauma becomes normalized,

Those who try to break the cycle falls into the trap of ridicule.

Pain soon follows

But you do not understand,

How can you?

You're also numbed by the same insecurities in only a

different attire,

Repressed and suppressed coming up in opposing forces,

To convince yourself, "it's all fine."

When pain is only a natural response to a failed system.

You put pills in my mouth and check my vitals,

Not knowing the failed system has murdered me already,

Not knowing insanity is sanity in a world we're living in.

Before the war comes

The war will commence tomorrow.

Army tanks, and loaded guns would bloom in place of flowers

in my garden.

The button has been pressed.

The news says they'd nuke us all up, it's only a matter of days,

In my homeland.

So I write my epitaph for none to read,

Unless aliens come invade us,

Anything can happen.

Ma, i forgive you.

Pa, i love you.

And i drink twenty bottles of alcohol

While the war comes to knock at my backdoor,

I laugh and watch my childhood cartoon shows,

And it all ends soon,

So I play with my toys and dance in a feral joy.

No one will be alive to miss no one else.

The war will commence tomorrow.

And I spend my last moments giddy in a manic haze,

Darling, would you join me while stars from night sky fall down upon us,

One by one

While we kiss,

Blood dripping down our cracked skulls?

When the world closes its eyes

And then the lights turn off, candles burn out,

The flames around hearts fade out,

In one swish of the wind,

The world closes its eyes.

Flames arise not out of a matchstick,

But in the rubbles that hide

A hundred pairs of beady eyes,

Extending one burnt hand to the sky.

The world closes its eyes,

Numbed down to a blissful nothingness

While the poison drips down burning their throats, stomach, insides.

Forty five pieces of conscience- we swallow them down

With two tranquilizers.

The burnt-leaves that harbours the burnt out cracker

Is only a collateral damage

Stained in blood, panic in eyes,

Only the world closes its eyes,

Like God when blood overpowers.
When the wick burns out
Laced in crimson blood
The absence of light begs you to close your eyes
Like in a night-time slumber
When the world closes its eyes.

For the candle of dreams

They stripped bare the light from a candle of dreams,
Staining freshly bloomed flowers with blood
Rebels outside were too busy fighting amongst themselves
And for causes - shallow and bland.
It's time to close your eyes, isn't it, when the final thud echoes?
You write slogans on walls in expired spray paint
And they carve cuts round a fresh flesh,
Oh a new prey! How delicious!
It's time to zip your mouth that promised to shout loud,
When the naked truth ensues, isn't it?

Here, lies a cavern of soft bed of flowers
For all the naked candles of dreams,
Their lights snatched away
too soon to fathom.
Flowers rot, corpses decay, memories haunt
And a mother cries,

While your jests take lives.
Oh no! But all they see is a new prey, don't you?

Two sides of the same coin

Through the rubbles and the dust,
Admist the shameless silence and nameless faces,
Rises a single stalk of flower in the voice of a child
Singing a single lullaby,-
A lullaby that rises above the warplanes,
Diffusing in the grey smoke of demolished homes.
The darkness of a cold world that watches with closed eyes,
Caves in to the beam of a single voice singing
Amidst the screams and the bombs.
Two sides of the same coin, of humanity
Where one side cares for the deceased unknown
And another pledges to destroy more and more,
Flip and toss in front of an absurd sky
Echoing the voice of a child
Singing a single lullaby.

Through the bloodstained clothes,
Amidst the thirsty cries and the thirst for blood,
Shoots a single beam of light in the smile of a child

That knows not to stop dreaming of an open sky
That doesn't rain missiles, -
Missiles that strike away the smile
Stripping some naked off of their humanity.
The smile rages on, through thick and thin,
Through the bombs and army tanks,
It rises like a flame in the place of fires
Like a single star that guides the sailor.
Two sides of the same coin,
Where one side comforts a grieving stranger
And another kills infants in daylight,
Flip and toss under the absurd sky
Beaming a single smile.

A genocide and the mountains

Bloodstains on an indifferent mountain

Lay as a single memoir of a genocide,

Where cries of a human child get lost amidst a sharp silence.

Corpses lay frozen buried under snow,

Whose lives flick away like a speck of dust into the sombre sky.

The sky doesn't flinch; the bare mountains do not bat an eye.

The obstinate river rushes through,

The predator chases the prey,

The stone cold heart of rocky mountains beat on despite.

The oppressed and the oppressor runs from the same landslide of a nonchalant terrain.

The ravishing mountains do not discriminate between the killer and the killed.

Frost bites everyone regardless.

Its solemn silence pierces through the fragility of human existence.

The rocks do not keep score of who has survived and who hasn't.

Tears pouring into the streams

Lay as a single memoir of a genocide

Where the impassive sky still lights up in stars over a thousand dead bodies.

After all, from a distance, the dead and the living looks just the same.

Under the sky, we're all directionless ants

Searching for the same sugary peace.

In the face of an unbothered cosmos,

The oppressed and the oppressor has to hold each other's hands

To not trip over the edge of the precipice.

Only in the night, when the moon shines up above like a fancy ornament

You can hear the mountains laugh at a genocide

Entertained enough by this foolish bickering.

My dear mother nature

My womanhood slips in

through the cracks on Earth's crusts,

Decaying and degrading

like a starving deer in a decapitated forest.

My heart, already labeled to be too fragile,

burns like forest fires.

It burns in rage against the void,

until it melts like ice caps.

It rises like the sea level

drowning homes of love you and I dream of only.

The void keeps calm, not a word,

when Mother Nature gets raped over again and again

And her children too busy to care for a terminally ill mother.

Little do I know,

when I flicked the butts of cigarettes into the drain,

That the microplastics only build a cancer in her body,

While i scream in a make-believe world of protests.

Mother Nature, my body was not born to be mine,

Just like yours,

Do we only connect through chaos and destruction,

While the mercury in retrograde rises in the thermometer?

Do we only kiss each other

when our births were pre-destined to be a decor only,

Tell me, oh tell me, before the green in my eyes turn brown.

Before the green in your chest turns into concrete.

Before we both burn in a pier of dry logs.

But you rise like a flame admist the petroleum on the ocean,

Changing and evolving into an angry madness.

So, don't forget I am your daughter,

The flames in my uterus reaches my head too

And i promise to lay my hand gently on your red eyes,

Before the world caves in,

Until they finally look at all the damage undone,

Oneday, I promise you Mother,

my dear Mother Nature.

After the storm

What happens after the storm?

Does the Sun come out and light everything up?

The sky pretending to have no idea what happened yesterday -

Like the gatekeeper of an ailing nation.

Do you feel the steady breeze? -

calm and tender,

Brushing your forehead

checking your temperament

to see,

if your insides are still hot from the rage and desperation of losing and fearing.

They bribe you with the day after the storm

'cause they fear you.

They fear your rage.

Your tears.

Your cries of help.

Your disappointment.

They know well how this rage, tears, cries, disappointment would boil up a nasty strong potion that would burn their invisible emperor's clothes.

How that would pierce through their skin revealing the naked lies underneath.

So they gift you the day after the storm.

Like a candy to a child who saw you kill.

Or a bone to the dog who saw you trespass.

A bandaid on a fracture.

An eerie welcoming cemetery

Death meets time while crossing moss-ridden derelict paths,

Birthing cracked tombstones - grey and green;

An attempt at immortalization;

To commemorate the last dying gasp to suck in life,

Only to fail.

A life of morbid yearns and cherry romance buries under sheaths of dead leaves-

Only to create another home to spiders and ants,

Birds and squirrels, -

Taking over human existence; -

An intra-species transcendence.

Abandonment and reclamation meets hand in hand in a parthenon of weary columns,

As time rustles through the solemn, silent trees.

Sounds of life changes medium from laughters and wails,

To crickets chirping,

Echoing and amplifying the hollow void of death over and over again.

I touch the ancient stone,

And in a whirlpool of turbulent passing ages,

I oscillate between past, present and future,

I reside and rest in the blurry lines in between them.

An array of emotions lies in its primitive form, -

Their dry bones and misty ghosts lie hooked on to the ridges and pores -

Painted over and under a decaying glory.

Braids of riddled visions shoot out of my mouth, my eyes,

Finding resonance in an empty cemetery in a strange afternoon,

Circling and gyrating over and around.

Deaths you can perceive and deaths that escape conscious sense,

Clasps hands in a manic dance;

Shifting in and out of conscious focus.

I turn my head to catch a glimpse,

They are gone destined to only be seen through the side of my eyes, -

a passing imagery.

Everything that matters in a bustling city light,

When cars rush past and people walk steadfast to an immediate destination,

Melts into a damp wetness below a crooked branching old tree,

Beside tombstones of faded grief,

Of the desire to never face the most inevitable of all inevitability.

The sky shades over it all in a steady shifting pattern.

It's a portal to an indifferent cosmos.

Except the nonchalant indifference is a wide open embrace to me,

That calms me,

Excites me,

Simultaneously.

The sea tastes like tears

The sea tastes like tears on my thirsty tongue,

Its waves fling on my scathed body,

Stripping me bare off all the cautious disguise I put on,

On lonely delirious nights.

The sea tastes like blood on my cracked lips,

Its currents tug at my frail feet,

Shifting the sand from the clogged pores of my lungs

That scuffles to inhale.

The sea cries at my knees hugging my calves,

And I cry with her -

Our tears join in a fragile estuary and I see it all in my tastebuds -

How the sea tastes like my tears and your tears and all the tears -

The unseen, fiery tears that dripped down in a quiet rage from a painful autoclave in our hearts,

And evaporated up into the welcoming arms of a clear sky.

The sea holds my hand and tumbles me over and in her sceptic eyes,

Her anger ebbs out, I see a collage of pain and loss, -

An abode of tears deep in sombre contemplation.
The sea tastes like tears in my five senses and a sixth,
And I embrace her under the furious waves,
Where her anger is not there to protect her anymore.

A realization

Pure and tender in its mellow blue shine,
The sky looks down upon me,
Like a curious child inspecting sand in their feet,
Except I'm the sand,
One tiny grain on its rough texture,
A universe locked in me,
Connected to a million other Universes out there,
Knowingly and unknowingly.

Dew drops on leaves in potted plants,
Reflect the entire sky in its tiny dome,
Like perception of a vague cryptic sensation,
Except I'm biased,
In my own trail of neural pathways,
A desire to be more than oneself,
A realization, huge and majestic like a galaxy,
Bursting and fuming.

The oblivion

Between thick foliages of moist darkness,

A still silence breathes cautiously.

A wooden window with cold drapes frames a very generic scene,

Of misty haze wrapped in sombre shades,

In sheaths of mountains plastered in shadows and leaking sunshine,

Dangerous beauty like Medusa's gaze,

Secrets and mysteries lurk between its peaceful trees.

Clouds make delicate blankets,

That gurgle over gorges and canyons,

Into a familiar snow capped picturesque range,

Known so much, yet so little.

Somewhere beyond them,

Through the skies of grey and blue,

My breath travels into the oblivion,

Too far gone to be called for.

Each vibration of the beating of my heart,

Tweaks into a clandestine storm

Much deeper into the oblivion,

Their contemptuous indifference stings my skin,
As I stare and dissolve into the oblivion.

I exist since the beginning of time

My frail legs hold this form,

At the edge of a moss ridden precipice,

Beside a canyon steeping low to rise high

Against the gigantic universe,

Like a warrior before it's last breath,

The mountains and I - are we much different?

I feel my existence boil and fry in front of Earth's broken crusts

Turned into a mayhem of jarred madness,

Contrasts and similarities in sheer prominence

Loom up high through my bones and veins,

Exhales out of my mouth in eerie spirals of steam,

That once constituted the ground I stand on.

I'm a small motiff on an intricate stitchwork in an expanding universe.

The atoms on my heart have travelled a long way,

Through rapids, and cities, and grass, and butterflies,

And lights and heat and air and dreams,

I'm only a compilation of all these snow,

Rain and coffee, smiles and feathers, boulders and

twigs.

This form is a train,

Transporting pieces of stories and identity,

To a graveyard, in a crematorium,

To come back as another small motiff on these mountains that hold me,

The moments that keep me running this train.

I'm only a heap of interactive atoms,

Seperated and connected through and beyond my lifetime,

With or without an illusion of consciousness,

I exist since the beginning of time.

About the Author

Chaaru Bhattacharyya

Chaaru Bhattacharyya (they/them) uses poetry as a refuge to seek shelter from internal and external conflicts. Writing from an young age, they derive peace from translating their thoughts and emotions into words. The author writes in the hope that we may connect fragility to fragility.

www.ingramcontent.com/pod-product-compliance
Lightning Source LLC
LaVergne TN
LVHW041629070526
838199LV00052B/3296